BALCONY GARDENING FOR BEGINNERS

Dr. Penny Watson

TABLE OF CONTENTS

CHAPTER ONE

Getting Started with Balcony Gardening

Imagine stepping out onto your balcony each morning, greeted by the soothing sight of lush greenery, vibrant blooms, and the invigorating scent of fresh herbs.

The idea of transforming your small outdoor space into a thriving garden oasis may seem like a distant dream, but the reality is that balcony gardening is not only possible; it's a delightful and rewarding endeavor that's accessible to everyone, regardless of your gardening experience or the size of your balcony.

Balcony gardening offers an opportunity to bring nature closer to home, even in the heart of a bustling city. Whether you reside in an urban apartment or a suburban townhouse, cultivating a mini paradise on your balcony allows you to reconnect with the natural world, reduce stress, and embrace the joys of nurturing life, all within the confines of your own private outdoor sanctuary.

This chapter marks the beginning of your exciting journey into the world of balcony gardening. It's an exploration of possibilities, a guide to overcoming challenges, and a source of inspiration that will help you create a verdant haven in the sky. Even if you've never planted a single seed or if you've only dabbled in gardening before, this book is here to offer you the knowledge, tools, and encouragement you need to flourish as a balcony gardener.

The Benefits of Balcony Gardening

As we begin this journey, we'll delve into the countless advantages of balcony gardening. From the tangible benefits like access to fresh, homegrown produce, to the intangible rewards such as improved mental well-being, the balcony garden is a source of both practicality and joy.

Assessing Your Balcony Space

Every balcony is unique, and understanding the nuances of your particular space is crucial. In this section, we'll explore how to evaluate your balcony, taking into account factors like size, orientation, and environmental conditions, to determine its gardening potential.

Choosing the Right Containers and Soil

The choice of containers and soil is pivotal in ensuring your plants thrive. Here, you'll discover how to select the most suitable containers for your garden, as well as the importance of high-quality soil to nurture your plants' roots.

Selecting Suitable Plants for Your Balcony

Not all plants are created equal when it comes to balcony gardening. We'll guide you through the process of choosing the right plants that are well-suited to your balcony's conditions and your personal preferences.

Understanding Sunlight and Microclimates

Sunlight is the lifeblood of plants, and it's vital to comprehend the sunlight patterns on your balcony. We'll also discuss microclimates, which can vary significantly even within a small outdoor space, and how they impact plant selection and placement.

The Benefits of Balcony Gardening

Urban living often means limited access to nature, and as our cities grow, green spaces can become increasingly scarce. However, this doesn't mean that nature and gardening are entirely out of reach. Balcony gardening is a delightful and practical way to bring the natural world closer to our urban lives. It offers a plethora of benefits that extend beyond the simple act of growing plants.

1. Connecting with Nature:

One of the most significant benefits of balcony gardening is the opportunity it provides to reconnect with nature. In a world that's becoming increasingly digitized, spending time in your balcony garden allows you to experience the sights, sounds, and scents of the natural world. It's a soothing and meditative experience, offering a reprieve from the hustle and bustle of city life.

2. Stress Reduction:

Research has shown that interacting with plants and nature can have a calming effect on the human psyche. Balcony gardening can serve as a form of therapy, helping to reduce stress and anxiety.

The simple act of tending to your plants, feeling the soil in your hands, and watching your garden flourish can be a therapeutic escape from the demands of everyday life.

3. Improved Air Quality:

Plants are natural air purifiers. They absorb carbon dioxide and release oxygen, improving the air quality around your balcony and, indirectly, in your living space. Balcony gardens can help filter out pollutants and create a fresher, more invigorating atmosphere for you to enjoy.

4. Fresh, Homegrown Produce:

With a well-planned balcony garden, you can grow a variety of herbs, vegetables, and even fruits. Imagine stepping out to pick a handful of fresh basil or ripe cherry tomatoes for your evening salad. Homegrown produce is not only more flavorful but also free from the pesticides and chemicals that can be present in store-bought options.

5. Enhanced Aesthetics:

Balcony gardens are a visual delight. They add color, texture, and life to your outdoor space, making it more inviting and aesthetically pleasing.

Whether you prefer a vibrant, flowery display or a serene green oasis, you have the freedom to design your garden to match your personal style.

6. Learning and Growth:

Balcony gardening is a fantastic opportunity for personal growth. It's a hobby that encourages learning, problem-solving, and patience. As you care for your plants, you'll acquire knowledge about different species, their growth cycles, and the intricacies of gardening. It's a journey of continual discovery.

7. Encourages Sustainable Living:

Gardening, even on a small scale, promotes sustainability. By growing your own produce, you reduce your reliance on store-bought items that may be transported long distances, thereby lowering your carbon footprint. Additionally, composting kitchen waste and using eco-friendly gardening practices contribute to a more sustainable lifestyle.

8. Creative Outlet:

Balcony gardening is a creative outlet that allows you to express yourself through plant selection, arrangement, and decor. It's an opportunity to experiment with design, colors, and textures, and to shape your outdoor space in a way that resonates with your personality.

9. Connection with the Seasons:

Through balcony gardening, you become attuned to the changing seasons. You'll learn to adapt your gardening practices to the needs of your plants as the weather shifts. This connection to the seasons can provide a deeper appreciation for the natural world and a sense of time and continuity.

10. Community Building:

Balcony gardening can also be a conversation starter with neighbors and fellow garden enthusiasts. Sharing your experiences, knowledge, and even extra produce can foster a sense of community in your building or neighborhood.

Assessing Your Balcony Space

Balconies come in all shapes and sizes, each with its unique characteristics and challenges. Whether you have a spacious balcony that spans the length of your apartment or a cozy, narrow space, assessing your balcony is the crucial first step in your journey to create a thriving balcony garden.

Understanding your space's limitations and potential will help you make informed decisions about the layout, choice of plants, and overall design of your garden.

Size and Layout:

The size of your balcony is a fundamental factor that will influence your gardening choices. Smaller balconies may require more creative use of space, while larger ones offer greater flexibility.

Measure your balcony's dimensions, noting the length, width, and any irregularities like protruding walls or architectural features. Once you have these measurements, you can start planning how to best utilize the available area.

Consider the layout of your balcony as well. Is it a long, narrow space, or is it more square in shape? The layout will impact where you place containers, seating, and other elements within your garden. If your balcony has irregular angles or alcoves, these can be opportunities for unique design features or cozy nooks.

Orientation and Sunlight:

Understanding the orientation of your balcony is essential for successful gardening. The direction your balcony faces will determine the amount of sunlight it receives throughout the day. Different plants have varying light requirements, and knowing your balcony's orientation will help you choose plants that will thrive.

- **North-Facing Balconies:** These balconies receive the least direct sunlight and are often shaded for most of the day. Choose shade-tolerant plants like ferns, impatiens, or hostas for these spaces.
- **East-Facing Balconies:** East-facing balconies receive morning sun and afternoon shade. Many herbs, such as basil and parsley, thrive in this type of light.

- **South-Facing Balconies:** South-facing balconies typically get the most direct sunlight throughout the day. This is ideal for sun-loving plants like tomatoes, peppers, and succulents.
- **West-Facing Balconies:** West-facing balconies receive strong afternoon sun but may be shaded in the morning. Plants that can handle the heat, like lavender and rosemary, are excellent choices.

Environmental Conditions:

Take note of any environmental conditions that may affect your balcony garden. Is your balcony exposed to strong winds, or is it sheltered from them? Wind can quickly dry out soil and plants, so wind-exposed balconies may require more frequent watering.

Consider the microclimate on your balcony as well. The presence of nearby buildings, trees, or other structures can create pockets of shade or warmth. These microclimates can be leveraged to grow a wider variety of plants or to protect sensitive ones.

Access and Safety:

Ensure that your balcony is safe and accessible for gardening. Check the condition of the balcony floor and railings, and make any necessary repairs to ensure safety. Be mindful of weight limits for your balcony, especially if you plan to place heavy containers or large structures.

Access to water is another crucial aspect to consider. Make sure you have a convenient water source on your balcony or that you have a system in place for easy watering. This can include a watering can, hose, or a drip irrigation system.

Local Regulations:

Before diving into balcony gardening, be aware of any local regulations or building rules that may apply to your balcony. Some apartments or condominiums may have restrictions on the types of plants, containers, or structures allowed on balconies. It's essential to know and adhere to these regulations to avoid any issues with your building management or neighbors.

Choosing the Right Containers and Soil

Balcony gardening is a creative and rewarding endeavor, but its success often hinges on two critical factors: the choice of containers and the quality of soil. As your balcony is a confined space, making smart decisions in these areas is paramount to nurturing thriving plants and creating a visually appealing garden.

Containers

Selecting the appropriate containers for your balcony garden is crucial, as it directly impacts the well-being of your plants. The range of choices can be overwhelming, but several key considerations can help guide your decision.

1. Material: Containers come in various materials, each with its advantages and drawbacks. Terracotta and clay pots are classic choices, known for their breathability and aesthetic appeal. However, they tend to dry out quickly, so you'll need to water your plants more frequently. Plastic containers are lightweight and retain moisture better, making them suitable for heat-sensitive plants.

Wooden containers, such as cedar or redwood, have natural beauty and insulating properties. The choice of material should align with the needs of your plants and your personal preferences.

2. Size: The size of your containers should accommodate the root systems of the plants you intend to grow. Smaller containers are suitable for herbs or compact flowers, while larger containers are essential for vegetables or shrubs. Adequate space for root growth allows your plants to access the nutrients and moisture they need to thrive.

3. Drainage: Proper drainage is non-negotiable. Containers should have drainage holes at the bottom to prevent waterlogging. Without adequate drainage, roots may become waterlogged, leading to root rot and plant decline.

4. Aesthetics: While functionality is paramount, don't underestimate the importance of aesthetics. Your containers should complement your balcony's design and your personal style. Consider colors, shapes, and textures that enhance the overall visual appeal of your garden.

Soil

Choosing the right soil for your balcony garden is equally important. Unlike garden beds, where plants can root deeply and access a wealth of nutrients, balcony gardens rely on the soil you provide. Here's what you need to consider:

1. Container Mix: Potting mixes, designed specifically for containers, are readily available and are ideal for balcony gardening. They are lightweight, well-draining, and provide essential nutrients for potted plants. Avoid using garden soil, as it tends to become compacted and lacks the necessary drainage.

2. Fertilization: Container plants rely on you for their nutrition. Choose a potting mix that contains slow-release fertilizers or incorporate your own as needed. Regular feeding is essential, as container plants quickly deplete the available nutrients in the soil.

3. pH Levels: The pH level of your soil can influence nutrient availability to your plants. Most plants prefer a slightly acidic to neutral pH. Test your soil's pH and adjust it if necessary using additives like lime or sulfur.

4. Moisture Retention: Balcony gardens can dry out quickly, especially in hot weather. Consider adding moisture-retaining amendments like peat moss or coconut coir to your potting mix. These materials help the soil retain moisture and reduce the need for frequent watering.

5. Mulch: A layer of mulch on the surface of your containers can further help with moisture retention, reduce weed growth, and maintain a more stable soil temperature.

Tips for Success

- **Repot as Needed:** As your plants grow, they may outgrow their containers. Repotting into larger containers ensures that their roots have sufficient space to expand and take up nutrients.

- **Seasonal Considerations:** Different seasons can impact the moisture and temperature of your soil. Adjust your watering schedule and consider using insulating materials during colder months to protect your plants from frost.

- **Regular Monitoring:** Keep an eye on the condition of your containers and soil. Check for signs of root-bound plants, nutrient deficiencies, or pests, and address issues promptly.

Selecting Suitable Plants for Your Balcony

One of the most exciting aspects of balcony gardening is the vast array of plant choices available to you. From fragrant flowers to culinary herbs, and even small fruit-bearing trees, your balcony can become a thriving haven for a diverse range of plants. However, choosing the right plants is essential for the success of your balcony garden.

1. Assess Your Balcony's Conditions:
Before you start selecting plants, it's crucial to consider the conditions of your balcony, as they will play a significant role in determining which plants will thrive:

- **Sunlight:** Determine how much sunlight your balcony receives throughout the day. Is it a sunny spot, partially shaded, or mostly in the shade? Most plants have specific light requirements, so matching them to your balcony's sunlight is essential.

- **Microclimates:** Be aware of any microclimates on your balcony. Areas near walls or structures may be warmer or colder, and some spots might be windier or more sheltered. Understanding these microclimates will help you select the right plants for each location.
- **Wind Exposure:** Wind can be a challenge for balcony gardening. If your balcony is particularly windy, consider wind-resistant plants or use windbreaks to protect more delicate species.

2. Consider the Size of Your Balcony:

The size of your balcony will determine the number and types of plants you can accommodate. In a small space, opt for compact or dwarf varieties, or use vertical gardening techniques to maximize the use of vertical space. Larger balconies offer more flexibility, allowing you to grow a variety of plants and even create distinct garden zones.

3. Think About Plant Compatibilities:

Consider how your chosen plants will coexist on your balcony. Do they have similar water, light, and nutrient requirements?

Will they complement each other aesthetically? Think about the visual and functional relationships between the plants you select.

4. Choose Plants You Love:

Your balcony garden is an extension of your living space, and it should reflect your personal tastes. Choose plants that you genuinely love and enjoy caring for. Whether you prefer the vibrant colors of flowers, the fragrance of herbs, or the utility of edible plants, your garden should bring you joy.

5. Match Plants to Your Gardening Experience:
Your level of gardening experience should also guide your plant selection. If you're new to gardening, start with easy-to-care-for plants like succulents, herbs, or resilient flowering annuals. If you're an experienced gardener, you can experiment with more challenging species.

6. Edible vs. Ornamental Plants:
Decide if you want to focus on growing edible plants like herbs, vegetables, or fruits, or if you prefer ornamental plants for their visual appeal.Many plants can serve both purposes, such as ornamental peppers that produce colorful, edible fruits.

7. Be Mindful of Toxic Plants:

If you have pets or small children, research potential toxicity of the plants you choose. Avoid plants that can be harmful if ingested, and opt for pet- and child-safe varieties.

8. Longevity and Seasonal Variability:

Consider whether you want to grow annuals, perennials, or a mix of both. Annuals provide vibrant color for a single season, while perennials can offer long-lasting beauty. A combination of both allows for changing displays and a dynamic balcony garden.

9. Pots and Containers:

Choose the right-sized containers for your selected plants. Some plants require larger pots, while others can thrive in smaller ones. Ensure that the containers have adequate drainage to prevent overwatering.

10. Practical Considerations:

Lastly, think about the practical aspects of maintaining your balcony garden. Will you have the time and resources for regular watering, fertilizing, and pruning? Select plants that align with your maintenance capabilities.

Understanding Sunlight and Microclimates

One of the most critical aspects of successful balcony gardening is comprehending how sunlight and microclimates impact your outdoor space. Just like in the natural world, the amount and quality of sunlight your plants receive can greatly influence their growth and well-being.

Sunlight: The Life Force for Your Plants

Sunlight is the primary source of energy for plants. It powers the process of photosynthesis, in which plants convert sunlight into sugars and oxygen, enabling them to grow, produce flowers, and bear fruit. When planning your balcony garden, consider these key aspects of sunlight:

1. Sunlight Exposure:

Balconies can vary significantly in terms of their exposure to sunlight. Understanding the sunlight patterns on your balcony is essential for selecting the right plants. Here are the main categories of sunlight exposure:

- **Full Sun:** Balconies that receive direct sunlight for most of the day are considered full sun locations. They typically get at least 6 hours of direct sunlight daily. Plants that thrive in full sun include tomatoes, peppers, and sunflowers.

- **Partial Sun/Partial Shade:** Balconies with a mix of direct sunlight and shade throughout the day fall into this category. Many flowering annuals and herbs, such as petunias and basil, do well in partial sun conditions.

- **Full Shade:** Some balconies, due to their orientation or nearby buildings, may receive minimal to no direct sunlight. Shade-loving plants like ferns, impatiens, and hostas are ideal for these areas.

2. Sun Angles and Intensity:

The angle of the sun in the sky changes throughout the day and over the course of the year. It's essential to consider how the sun's angle affects your balcony. During the summer, the sun is higher in the sky and may cast different shadows than in the winter when it's lower. Balconies with southwestern exposure, for example, may receive intense afternoon sun in the summer but be less sunny in the winter.

Microclimates: The Balcony's Unique Zones

Microclimates are localized climate variations that can exist within a small space, such as your balcony. Understanding these microclimates is key to selecting the right plants and optimizing growing conditions:

1. Temperature Variations:

The temperature on your balcony can vary significantly due to factors like shade, wind, and the presence of nearby structures. South or west-facing balconies often receive more heat, while north or east-facing ones may be cooler. Use this knowledge to choose plants that are well-suited to your balcony's temperature range.

2. Wind and Shelter:

Wind can have a considerable impact on your plants. Windy balconies can cause soil to dry out faster, and some plants may struggle to withstand strong winds. Using windbreaks, like trellises or tall plants, can provide shelter for more delicate species.

3. Sheltered and Sunny Spots:

Different areas of your balcony may offer varying levels of shelter and sunlight. South-facing walls or corners may receive more sunlight and warmth, while areas near walls or other structures could be shadier and cooler. These microclimates create opportunities for growing different types of plants in distinct zones.

4. Reflective Surfaces:

Surfaces like glass or concrete can reflect sunlight and heat, creating localized microclimates. Be aware of how these surfaces impact the conditions on your balcony, as they can contribute to temperature extremes or increased light.

5. Seasonal Changes:

Microclimates can shift with the seasons. What's a sunny, warm spot in the summer may become shaded and cooler in the winter. Understanding these seasonal variations can help you adapt your plant selection and care routine accordingly.

CHAPTER TWO

Essential Tools and Materials

Now that you've embarked on your journey into balcony gardening, you're ready to dive deeper into the heart of this green endeavor. Balcony gardening offers an opportunity to bring life and beauty to your outdoor space, but to do so effectively, you'll need a set of essential tools and materials. This chapter is your guide to the equipment and supplies that will help you nurture your plants, maintain your garden, and ensure a thriving and aesthetically pleasing balcony garden.

Balcony gardening, much like traditional gardening, requires a degree of preparation and care, and the right tools and materials are your trusty companions in this horticultural adventure. They are the instruments that will help you sow the seeds of your vision, cultivate a green oasis, and harvest the joys of your labor.

As we delve into the world of essential tools and materials for balcony gardening, you'll discover that these elements are more than mere accessories; they are the essential building blocks of your success.

They will empower you to design your garden, maintain its health, and overcome the challenges that arise along the way.

From the simplest hand tools to advanced irrigation systems, from the basic potting mix to specialized fertilizers, we will explore the variety of options available to you. The choices you make will depend on the scale of your balcony garden, the types of plants you wish to nurture, and your personal preferences.

The Toolbox of a Balcony Gardener

As a balcony gardener, your toolbox should be a carefully curated collection of instruments designed to make your gardening tasks more efficient and enjoyable. Whether you're a novice gardener or have a seasoned green thumb, having the right tools is essential. This toolbox includes the following:

- **Hand Tools:** Hand trowels, pruners, shears, weeding tools, and a good pair of gloves are indispensable for planting, transplanting, pruning, and maintaining your plants.

- **Watering Equipment:** A watering can or hose, as well as a spray nozzle or drip irrigation system, will help you deliver the right amount of water to your plants while preventing overwatering or soil erosion.
- **Containers:** The right selection of pots and containers is crucial. You'll need various sizes and materials to accommodate different plant types and sizes.
- **Soil and Soil Amendments:** Potting mix, organic matter like compost or peat moss, and amendments like perlite or vermiculite will provide the foundation for your plants to grow.
- **Fertilizers and Nutrients:** Whether you choose slow-release granular fertilizers, liquid plant food, or organic compost, providing the right nutrients is essential for your plants' growth and health.
- **Pest and Disease Control:** Insect repellents, organic remedies, or protective netting can help prevent and address common pest and disease issues.
- **Support Structures:** Trellises, stakes, and cages are useful for supporting climbing plants or helping upright plants stay sturdy in the wind.

- **Mulch:** A layer of mulch can help with moisture retention, weed control, and temperature regulation for your containers.
- **Decor and Accessories:** Plant labels, garden markers, decorative stones, and garden ornaments can add personal touches and enhance the aesthetics of your balcony garden.

Tailoring Your Toolkit

Your choice of tools and materials will depend on your unique needs and the scope of your balcony garden. Whether you're aiming for a vibrant, blooming balcony filled with flowers, a mini herb garden, or a green sanctuary with shrubs and trees, you can tailor your toolkit to suit your goals.

Gardening Tools You'll Need

Balcony gardening is a delightful and rewarding venture, and to make the most of it, you'll need the right set of gardening tools. Just as a chef relies on quality knives and utensils, a balcony gardener depends on a well-equipped toolbox to ensure the success of their green haven.

1. Hand Trowel:

A hand trowel is a versatile tool that you'll use for a variety of tasks, from planting seedlings and bulbs to transferring soil and compost. It allows for precise digging and helps maintain proper spacing between plants in your containers.

2. Pruners/Shears:

Pruners or shears are vital for maintaining the health and appearance of your plants. Whether it's trimming back overgrown foliage, removing dead or diseased branches, or harvesting herbs and flowers, a sharp pair of pruners is a must.

3. Weeding Tools:

Weeds can be persistent and can quickly invade your garden. Hand weeders or weed knives are essential for removing unwanted plants and keeping your balcony garden neat and healthy.

4. Garden Gloves:

Garden gloves not only protect your hands from dirt and potential scratches but also provide a better grip on tools and help prevent blisters. Choose a comfortable pair that fits well.

5. Watering Can or Hose:

A watering can with a fine spout is useful for precise watering, especially in containers. Alternatively, if you have access to a hose, consider using a spray nozzle to control water flow and minimize soil erosion in your pots.

6. Dibber:

A dibber is a pointed tool used for making holes in the soil to plant seeds or small seedlings at the correct depth. It ensures your plants get off to a strong start and minimizes root disturbance during planting.

7. Soil Scoop or Shovel:

A soil scoop or small shovel is invaluable for transferring soil, compost, or potting mix into containers and for scooping soil out for replanting or transplanting.

8. Garden Apron:

While not a tool in the traditional sense, a garden apron with pockets can be incredibly practical. It provides a convenient place to carry small tools, plant markers, and seeds, keeping everything you need close at hand.

9. Garden Markers:

Keeping track of what you've planted is essential for organizing your garden. Use plant markers to label your containers, ensuring you can identify your plants as they grow and change.

10. Soil Moisture Meter:

A soil moisture meter is a handy gadget for gauging the moisture level in your containers. It takes the guesswork out of watering, preventing overwatering or underwatering.

11. Soil pH Test Kit:

Measuring the pH of your soil is essential for understanding its acidity or alkalinity. Different plants have varying pH preferences, so a pH test kit helps you make adjustments for optimal plant health.

12. Garden Kneeler or Cushion:

Balcony gardening often involves kneeling or sitting for extended periods. A garden kneeler or cushion provides comfort and support, reducing strain on your knees and back.

13. Trowel Sharpener:

To keep your hand trowel, pruners, and other cutting tools in optimal condition, a trowel sharpener is a valuable addition to your toolkit. Sharp tools make tasks more efficient and reduce the risk of injuring your plants.

14. Tool Caddy or Garden Bag:

A tool caddy or garden bag helps you keep your gardening tools organized and easily accessible. It's a practical way to carry your tools and supplies from one end of your balcony to the other.

15. Garden Cart or Wheelbarrow:

If you have a larger balcony garden or need to transport heavy bags of soil or mulch, a garden cart or wheelbarrow can be a lifesaver. They make the task of moving materials much more manageable.

Fertilizers and Nutrient Management

Balcony gardening is a unique and rewarding way to cultivate your favorite plants in a confined urban space. To achieve lush and vibrant growth, one of the essential aspects to consider is nutrient management through fertilizers. Properly feeding your balcony plants with the right fertilizers is crucial for their health and productivity

The Role of Nutrients in Plant Growth:

Plants require essential nutrients to grow, and they obtain these nutrients from the soil or growing medium. These nutrients can be broadly categorized into two groups: macronutrients and micronutrients.

Macronutrients

1. Nitrogen (N): Nitrogen is essential for leafy growth, making it vital for the development of lush foliage. It's crucial for green, healthy leaves, and its deficiency can result in stunted growth and yellowing of foliage.

2. Phosphorus (P): Phosphorus is key for root development, flowering, and fruiting. It promotes strong root systems and helps plants produce vibrant flowers and fruits.

3. Potassium (K): Potassium is important for overall plant health. It enhances the plant's resistance to disease and stress, regulates water uptake, and supports photosynthesis.

Micronutrients

1. Iron (Fe): Iron is crucial for chlorophyll production, and its deficiency leads to yellowing leaves (chlorosis).

2. Magnesium (Mg): Magnesium plays a role in photosynthesis and overall plant metabolism.

3. Zinc (Zn), Copper (Cu), Manganese (Mn), and others: These micronutrients are required in smaller quantities but are essential for various metabolic functions in plants.

The Role of Fertilizers

In balcony gardening, where plants are grown in containers, nutrients can become depleted more quickly compared to in-ground gardens. As plants grow, they use up the available nutrients in the potting mix. Fertilizers replenish these nutrients, ensuring your plants have access to the elements they need to thrive.

Types of Fertilizers

1. Organic Fertilizers: Organic fertilizers, such as compost, well-rotted manure, and organic-based commercial products, release nutrients slowly as they decompose. They improve soil structure and microbial activity while nourishing your plants.

2. Inorganic or Synthetic Fertilizers: These are chemical-based fertilizers that provide nutrients in readily available forms. They are usually water-soluble and provide a quick nutrient boost to plants.

3. Controlled-Release Fertilizers: These fertilizers release nutrients gradually over an extended period, reducing the need for frequent applications.

Fertilizer Application

When using fertilizers in your balcony garden, it's crucial to follow best practices:

- **Read Labels:** Always read and follow the label instructions on the fertilizer product you choose. The label will provide information on the nutrient content, application rates, and timing.

- **Balanced Fertilizers:** Look for balanced fertilizers that provide a mix of essential macronutrients (N-P-K) and micronutrients. A balanced formulation ensures that all aspects of plant growth are supported.
- **Timing:** Apply fertilizers during the active growing season. Most plants benefit from regular feedings in spring and summer when they are actively growing. Reduce or cease feeding in fall and winter when plants are dormant.
- **Even Distribution:** Distribute fertilizers evenly across the surface of the potting mix, avoiding direct contact with plant stems or leaves. Water the plants after applying fertilizer to helnutrients penetrate the root zone.
- **Dilute Liquid Fertilizers:** If using liquid fertilizers, follow the recommended dilution rates to avoid over-fertilizing, which can damage plant roots.

Organic vs. Synthetic Fertilizers

The choice between organic and synthetic fertilizers is a matter of preference and consideration of your gardening philosophy. Both types have their advantages:

- **Organic Fertilizers:** Organic options improve soil structure, promote beneficial soil microorganisms, and are generally considered more environmentally friendly. They release nutrients slowly, reducing the risk of nutrient imbalances or over-fertilization.
- **Synthetic Fertilizers:** Synthetic fertilizers provide a quick nutrient boost and are easier to apply. They are formulated to deliver precise nutrient ratios. While they are efficient, overuse can lead to imbalances and nutrient runoff.

Balancing Nutrient Needs

Balcony gardeners should also be attentive to the specific nutrient needs of their plants. Different plant varieties have varying requirements, and it's essential to select fertilizers that match these needs. For example, leafy greens might benefit from a higher nitrogen fertilizer, while flowering plants require more phosphorus to support blooming.

Balcony gardeners can employ a combination of organic and synthetic fertilizers, depending on plant requirements and personal preferences.

Pest and Disease Control on the Balcony

Balcony gardening brings the beauty of nature to your urban space, but it also invites a few unwanted guests: pests and diseases. Managing these challenges is a critical aspect of maintaining a thriving balcony garden.

In this article, we will explore the importance of pest and disease control and strategies to keep your plants healthy.

Understanding the Threat: Pests and Diseases

Pests and diseases are common adversaries in gardening. They can quickly damage or even destroy your plants if left unaddressed. It's crucial to recognize the signs of an infestation or infection and take proactive steps to prevent and control these issues.

Common Pests

1. Aphids: These small, soft-bodied insects feed on plant sap, causing wilting, yellowing leaves, and a sticky substance called honeydew. They reproduce rapidly and can quickly infest your plants.

2. Whiteflies: Whiteflies are tiny, flying insects that feed on plant sap and can transmit plant diseases. They often swarm around infected plants and leave a white, powdery residue on leaves.

3. Spider Mites: These arachnids are so small they're almost invisible, but they can do significant damage. They suck the juices from plant cells, leaving stippled or discolored leaves.

4. Mealybugs: Mealybugs are small, white insects that produce a white, cottony substance. They feed on plant sap, causing wilting and yellowing of leaves.

5. Scale Insects: Scale insects attach themselves to plant stems and leaves, feeding on plant sap. They can be challenging to spot because they resemble small, flat bumps.

6. Slugs and Snails: These mollusks feed on plant leaves and can leave large, irregular holes in foliage.

Common Diseases

1. Powdery Mildew: Powdery mildew appears as a white, powdery substance on plant leaves. It can distort and weaken the affected foliage.

2. Leaf Spot: Leaf spot diseases cause small, round or irregularly shaped dark spots on leaves, which can coalesce and lead to leaf yellowing and death.

3. Root Rot: This disease affects the roots and causes wilting, yellowing, and poor plant growth. It is often caused by overwatering or poorly drained potting mix.

4. Botrytis (Gray Mold): Botrytis is a fungal disease that causes brown or gray mold on plant surfaces, often affecting flowers and fruit.

5. Damping Off: Damping off is a fungal disease that affects seedlings. It causes sudden wilting and collapse of young plants at or near the soil line.

Prevention and Control

Effective pest and disease control on the balcony begins with preventative measures and early intervention:

1. Healthy Plants
Start with healthy plants. Strong, vigorous plants are better equipped to fend off pests and diseases. Inspect new plants before adding them to your garden, as introducing infected plants can lead to issues down the road.

2. Proper Watering:

Overwatering can lead to root rot and other fungal diseases. Ensure your containers have good drainage, and water your plants based on their specific needs. Water in the morning to allow foliage to dry before evening, reducing the risk of fungal diseases.

3. Monitoring:

Regularly inspect your plants for signs of pests and diseases. Early detection allows for quicker intervention and can prevent issues from spreading.

4. Isolation:

If you notice a plant with signs of pests or diseases, isolate it from your other plants to prevent the issue from spreading.

5. Beneficial Insects:

Encourage the presence of beneficial insects, such as ladybugs, lacewings, and parasitoid wasps, which prey on common garden pests.

6. Natural Remedies:

Consider using natural remedies like neem oil, insecticidal soap, or horticultural oils to control pests. These solutions are less harmful to beneficial insects and the environment.

7. Organic and Chemical Controls:

For severe infestations or diseases, you may need to resort to organic or chemical controls. Always follow the label instructions and apply treatments carefully to minimize harm to the environment and beneficial organisms.

8. Pruning and Sanitation:

Regularly prune and remove infected or damaged plant parts. Clean your tools between plants to prevent disease transmission.

9. Crop Rotation:

If you grow vegetables, practice crop rotation to reduce the buildup of pests and diseases in the soil.

10. Quarantine:

Quarantine new plants for a few weeks before introducing them to your balcony garden. This allows you to monitor them for any signs of trouble before they interact with your existing plants.

Educate Yourself:

Balcony gardeners should take the time to educate themselves about common pests and diseases that affect their specific plants. Understanding the life cycles, symptoms, and preferred hosts of these problems can help you be more proactive and effective in your management efforts.

Watering Techniques and Irrigation Systems

In the world of balcony gardening, understanding the art of watering is a fundamental skill. Adequate and proper watering is the lifeline of your plants, as they rely on a consistent supply of moisture to thrive

1. Hand Watering:

Hand watering is the most straightforward and commonly used method in balcony gardening. It offers you the highest degree of control and allows you to observe your plants closely while providing the necessary moisture. Here are some tips for effective hand watering:

- **Use a Watering Can:** A watering can with a fine spout is ideal for precise watering. It helps prevent water from splashing onto leaves, which can lead to fungal issues.

- **Water at the Base:** Direct the water flow to the base of the plants to ensure that the roots receive adequate moisture.

- **Watering Schedule:** Determine the watering schedule based on the needs of your plants and the prevailing environmental conditions. Water in the morning to allow foliage to dry before evening, reducing the risk of fungal diseases.

- **Check Soil Moisture:** Before watering, check the soil moisture by inserting your finger into the potting mix. Water only if the top inch of soil feels dry.

2. Drip Irrigation Systems:

Drip irrigation systems are an excellent option for balcony gardeners who want to automate the watering process. These systems deliver water directly to the root zone, reducing water wastage and minimizing the risk of fungal diseases. Here's what you need to know about drip irrigation:

- **Drip Emitters:** Drip emitters or hoses with built-in emitters are used to deliver water precisely to each plant's root zone.
- **Timer:** A timer can be attached to your drip irrigation system to control when and how long it waters your plants.
- **Customization:** Drip systems can be customized to suit the layout of your balcony garden, ensuring that each plant receives the right amount of water.
- **Efficiency:** Drip systems are highly efficient, conserving water and reducing the risk of overwatering or underwatering.

3. Self-Watering Containers:

Self-watering containers are designed with a built-in water reservoir that allows plants to draw moisture as needed.

These containers are particularly helpful for those who may be away from their balcony garden for extended periods. Here's how self-watering containers work:

- **Reservoir:** The container has a separate water reservoir at the bottom, which is filled through a fill tube or designated opening.
- **Wicking Mechanism:** A wicking mechanism, such as a wick or soil capillary action, draws water from the reservoir into the potting mix as the plant's roots require it.
- **Water Level Indicator:** Some self-watering containers have a water level indicator, showing when it's time to refill the reservoir.

4. Capillary Matting:

Capillary matting is an effective, low-tech way to maintain consistent soil moisture. It consists of a mat placed beneath your containers, which draws water up to the potting mix via capillary action. Here's how it works:

- **Mat Placement:** The capillary mat is placed on a surface, and the containers are set on top of it.

- **Water Reservoir:** A water reservoir, like a tray or container, is placed below the matting, containing water.

- **Capillary Action:** The capillary mat draws water from the reservoir to the potting mix, ensuring a steady supply of moisture.

5. Water Globes or Spikes:

Water globes or spikes are decorative and practical tools for keeping plants hydrated. They are filled with water and slowly release it into the soil as the plant requires moisture. Here's how to use them:

- **Fill and Insert:** Fill the water globe or spike with water and insert it into the soil near the plant's roots.
- **Slow Release:** These devices release water slowly, preventing overwatering.

6. Wicking System:

A wicking system consists of a container with a wicking material, like a fabric strip or cord, that draws water from a reservoir up into the potting mix. It's a DIY solution that can be adapted to various container sizes.

- **Wicking Material:** The wicking material is partially submerged in a water reservoir and extends into the potting mix, ensuring a constant supply of moisture to the plants.

7. Soaker Hoses:

Soaker hoses are flexible hoses designed to ooze water along their entire length. They can be laid on the balcony surface or coiled around plants to deliver water directly to the root zone.

- **Efficiency:** Soaker hoses are efficient and minimize water wastage by directing moisture where it's needed most.

8. Spray Bottle or Misting:

For delicate or small plants, a spray bottle can be used to mist the foliage with water. Misting helps maintain humidity and can keep plants healthy, especially during hot and dry periods.

Seasonal Considerations for Balcony Gardening

Balcony gardening offers a unique opportunity to connect with nature and cultivate a green sanctuary in an urban environment. However, to be successful year-round, it's essential to consider the seasonal changes that affect your garden. Each season brings its own set of challenges and opportunities, and understanding these can help you maximize the beauty and productivity of your balcony garden.

Spring: The Season of Renewal

As spring unfolds, your balcony garden awakens from its winter slumber. This season offers an array of opportunities:

1. Planting New Life:

Spring is the ideal time for planting or replanting. As temperatures rise and daylight lengthens, plants come out of dormancy and start their growth. You can sow seeds, transplant seedlings, or refresh your container gardens with a variety of annuals, perennials, herbs, and vegetables.

2. Prepping for the Growing Season:

Spring is also the time to evaluate your garden's needs. Inspect your containers for wear and tear, replace any damaged ones, and refresh the potting mix. Fertilize your plants to provide them with the nutrients they need for the season ahead.

3. Watch for Frosts:

While spring brings warmth, it can also deliver unexpected frosts. Keep an eye on weather forecasts and be ready to protect your tender plants if a late frost is predicted.

Summer: The Season of Vigor

Summer is when your balcony garden is in full swing. However, this season presents some unique challenges:

1. Water Management:

As temperatures rise, plants often require more water. Be vigilant about watering your containers to prevent soil from drying out. Consider using mulch to help retain moisture and reduce evaporation.

2. Pest Control:

Warm weather can lead to increased pest activity. Keep a close watch for common garden pests and employ pest control measures as needed to protect your plants.

3. Sun and Shade:

Some plants may require shade during the hottest part of the day to prevent scorching. Use shade cloth or move containers to shadier spots as necessary.

4. Harvesting:

If you're growing vegetables or herbs, summer is the time for bountiful harvests. Enjoy the fresh produce from your balcony garden and consider preserving excess crops through freezing, drying, or canning.

Fall: The Season of Transition

Fall is a transitional season that requires careful management of your garden:

1. Cool-Season Crops:

As temperatures cool, shift your focus to cool-season crops like lettuce, kale, and spinach. These plants thrive in the milder fall weather.

2. Protect from Frost:

Keep an eye on temperature fluctuations and be prepared to protect your plants from early frosts. Use frost cloth or bring sensitive plants indoors overnight.

3. Plan for Winter:

Consider which plants you'd like to overwinter and make arrangements for storage, whether it's moving containers indoors, using cold frames, or wrapping them in insulating materials.

Winter: The Season of Rest

Winter is a time for your balcony garden to rest, but that doesn't mean you should neglect it:

1. Winterizing:

Take steps to winterize your garden, insulating your containers with mulch, bubble wrap, or other insulating materials to protect the root systems from freezing temperatures.

2. Evergreens and Perennials:

If you have evergreen plants or perennial herbs, they may continue to thrive during the winter. Keep an eye on their moisture needs and protect them from harsh winter winds.

3. Indoor Gardening:

Consider bringing a few of your favorite herbs or smaller potted plants indoors for a mini indoor garden during the winter months.

4. Planning for Spring:

While your garden rests, take the opportunity to plan and prepare for the coming spring. Research new plants, order seeds or supplies, and envision the layout of your garden for the upcoming growing season.

Year-Round Maintenance:

Regardless of the season, there are maintenance tasks that should be carried out year-round:

- Regularly inspect your plants for signs of pests or diseases.

  - Prune or deadhead as needed to encourage healthy growth.
  - Keep an eye on soil moisture and adjust your watering schedule as conditions change.
  - Provide support for plants that need it, such as trellises or stakes for climbers.
  - Remember to enjoy your balcony garden in every season. It's a place of tranquility and beauty no matter the time of year.

CHAPTER THREE

Designing Your Balcony Garden

Your balcony, whether spacious or compact, presents an incredible opportunity to connect with nature and design a green oasis in the heart of the urban jungle. Balcony gardening is a versatile and rewarding endeavor that allows you to cultivate a vibrant garden, no matter the size of your outdoor space. This introduction sets the stage for your journey into the world of balcony garden design, where we'll explore the principles, strategies, and creative techniques that will help you transform your balcony into a thriving and visually captivating garden.

In this bustling, fast-paced world, our outdoor spaces often provide a respite from the chaos of daily life. Balcony gardening, more than just a hobby, is a way to create a retreat that offers solace and serenity right at your doorstep.

Whether you live in a high-rise apartment, a cozy condominium, or any urban setting with a balcony, you can unlock the potential of your outdoor space and immerse yourself in the art of gardening.

The Balcony as a Canvas

Your balcony is a canvas awaiting your creative touch. Regardless of its size or layout, it possesses boundless potential for becoming a green paradise.

From the smallest balconies that can accommodate a few potted plants to more expansive spaces that allow for diverse landscaping, your balcony can be transformed into a place of beauty, tranquility, and inspiration.

Defying Space Limitations

One of the most compelling aspects of balcony gardening is its capacity to transcend spatial constraints. While traditional gardens are typically bound by the expanse of the ground, balcony gardens exist in a vertical world, allowing you to make the most of both floor and wall space.

This vertical dimension opens doors to various creative possibilities, from hanging gardens and trellises to vertical planters and shelving.

Your Unique Vision

Designing your balcony garden is a deeply personal endeavor. It's an opportunity to express your style, preferences, and personality through the arrangement of plants, colors, and decor.

As you embark on this journey, consider the ambiance you wish to create. Do you envision a serene retreat with aromatic herbs and calming colors, or a vibrant space bursting with flowering plants and vivid hues? The possibilities are as diverse as the individuals who embark on this adventure.

Planting a Purpose

Beyond aesthetics, your balcony garden can serve various purposes, depending on your goals and interests. Are you an aspiring gourmet chef who desires a bounty of herbs and vegetables at your fingertips?

Or perhaps you're a lover of fragrance, yearning for a space filled with aromatic blooms and herbs. Your balcony garden can also be a haven for pollinators, providing a vital refuge for bees and butterflies.

Bringing Nature Closer

In the hustle and bustle of urban life, we often find ourselves yearning for a closer connection to nature. Balcony gardening bridges this gap by allowing you to engage with the natural world daily.

Tending to your plants, observing their growth, and experiencing the changing seasons all contribute to a sense of fulfillment and well-being.

The Importance of Design:

Balcony garden design is about more than just arranging plants; it's a process of thoughtfully orchestrating elements to create a harmonious and balanced space. It involves considering the layout, selection of containers, choice of plants, color schemes, and the interplay of light and shade.

Effective design ensures that your garden not only looks beautiful but also functions optimally, fostering plant health and growth.

Environmental Impact:

As an urban gardener, your balcony can play a small but significant role in environmental conservation. Balcony gardens contribute to air purification, carbon sequestration, and urban heat reduction. They can also serve as important stepping stones for pollinators in an urban landscape.

Navigating Challenges:

Balcony gardening, like any form of gardening, has its unique challenges. From limited space and varying sunlight exposure to potential pest issues, these challenges are part of the journey. However, they can be overcome with knowledge, creative solutions, and a passion for plants.

Creating a Functional Layout

Designing a balcony garden is an exciting creative endeavor, but it's essential to strike a balance between aesthetics and functionality to ensure that your green haven is a practical and enjoyable space. Achieving a functional layout for your balcony garden involves careful planning and thoughtful decision-making.

1. Evaluate Your Space:

Before you start arranging plants and accessories, it's crucial to assess your balcony's size, shape, and layout. Consider the following aspects:

- **Dimensions:** Measure the width and depth of your balcony to determine the available planting and walking space.
- **Sunlight:** Note the direction in which your balcony faces and the amount of sunlight it receives throughout the day. This information is vital for selecting the right plants.
- **Access Points:** Identify doors, windows, or other openings that lead to the balcony. Ensure that your layout doesn't obstruct these entry points.
- **Safety Regulations:** Some apartment buildings have specific safety regulations regarding balconies, such as weight limits or restrictions on certain items. Familiarize yourself with these rules.

2. Define Zones:

To create a functional layout, it's helpful to divide your balcony into different zones based on their intended use. Common zones include:

- **Planting Zone:** This is the primary area for growing your plants. The type and number of containers you can place in this zone depend on the available space and sunlight.

- **Seating and Relaxation Zone:** Consider creating a comfortable space where you can sit, unwind, and enjoy your garden. This can be achieved with foldable chairs, cushions, and small tables.

- **Storage Zone:** Balconies often lack storage space. Incorporate storage solutions like cabinets, shelving, or storage benches to keep gardening tools, supplies, and pots organized.

- **Vertical Gardening Zone:** Utilize vertical space by adding wall-mounted planters, trellises, or shelves for growing plants vertically. This not only saves floor space but also adds visual interest.

3. Choose Suitable Containers:

Selecting the right containers is essential for a functional layout. Consider the following factors when choosing containers:

- **Size:** Containers should be appropriately sized for your plants. They should accommodate the root systems and allow room for growth.
- **Material:** Containers come in various materials, such as plastic, ceramic, terracotta, and fabric. Choose materials that complement your balcony's style and are suitable for your plant selection.
- **Drainage:** Ensure containers have adequate drainage holes to prevent overwatering. Elevate containers slightly to allow excess water to drain freely.

4. Plant Placement:

When arranging plants, keep the following principles in mind:

- **Grouping:** Cluster plants with similar water and sunlight requirements together. This simplifies maintenance and watering.

- **Layering:** Arrange taller plants at the back or in the center of your layout, with shorter plants in front or at the edges. This creates depth and ensures all plants receive sunlight.
- **Accessibility:** Place frequently used herbs or plants you want to showcase close to the seating area or walkway for easy access.

5. Seating and Decor:

Your balcony garden isn't just about plants; it's also a place for relaxation and enjoyment. Choose comfortable, space-saving seating options like foldable chairs or small benches. Enhance the ambiance with decorative elements such as cushions, outdoor rugs, lanterns, or wind chimes.

6. Shading and Privacy:

Consider adding shade solutions like umbrellas, pergolas, or shade cloth to protect yourself and your plants from intense sunlight. If privacy is a concern, use trellises, screens, or decorative partitions to create a more secluded and cozy atmosphere.

7. Maintenance and Access:

Ensure that your layout allows easy access to all areas for maintenance tasks like watering, pruning, and weeding. You should be able to reach all your plants without difficulty.

8. Lighting:

Don't forget about balcony lighting. Adequate lighting not only extends your enjoyment of the space into the evening but also adds to the safety and security of your balcony. Consider string lights, solar-powered lanterns, or wall-mounted fixtures.

9. Seasonal Adjustments:

Keep in mind that the layout may need to change with the seasons. Certain plants may require different light exposure at various times of the year. Be prepared to move containers or adjust your layout accordingly.

10. Safety:

Safety should always be a top priority. Ensure that your balcony garden layout doesn't create tripping hazards or obstruct emergency exits. Secure tall or heavy items to prevent them from falling in strong winds.

Vertical Gardening and Space Optimization

As urban living spaces continue to shrink, the need for creative gardening solutions has become more pressing than ever. Vertical gardening has emerged as a game-changing strategy, allowing urban dwellers to cultivate lush green oases on balconies, patios, and even indoors. This innovative approach not only maximizes space but also enhances aesthetics and promotes sustainability.

1. Vertical Gardening Unleashed:

Vertical gardening is a practice that involves growing plants vertically rather than horizontally. By utilizing walls, fences, trellises, shelves, and specially designed structures, you can transform your limited space into a thriving green haven. The concept isn't new; people have been training plants to grow upward for centuries.

However, modern urban gardening has taken vertical gardening to new heights, offering a wide range of possibilities.

2. Types of Vertical Gardens:

Vertical gardens come in various forms, each offering unique benefits and design options:

- **Green Walls:** These are large, living walls covered in an array of plants. They can be freestanding or mounted on existing structures and offer a striking visual impact.
- **Vertical Planters:** These are pockets, pouches, or panels specifically designed for vertical planting. They are attached to walls or structures and allow you to grow plants in individual compartments.
- **Trellises and Arbors:** Trellises and arbors provide support for climbing plants and can be customized to fit any space. They offer a blend of aesthetics and functionality.
- **Shelving and Ladder Gardens:** These are perfect for small balconies and patios. Utilize shelves or ladder-like structures to display a variety of potted plants.

- **Hanging Gardens:** Hanging planters and baskets are an excellent way to add greenery to small spaces. They can be hung from hooks, brackets, or rails.
- **Tower Gardens:** These are self-contained, vertical growing systems that allow you to cultivate a variety of plants in a small footprint.

3. Advantages of Vertical Gardening:

Vertical gardening offers several noteworthy advantages:

- **Space Maximization:** The most obvious benefit is the efficient use of space. Even the tiniest balconies can accommodate vertical gardens, allowing for an abundance of plants.
- **Aesthetic Appeal:** Vertical gardens are visually captivating and can transform a blank wall or uninviting space into a stunning, green focal point.
- **Privacy and Screening:** Vertical gardens can provide privacy and screening by creating natural barriers between your space and the outside world.

- **Reduced Maintenance:** Vertical gardens can be easier to maintain than traditional gardens because they minimize soil contact and reduce the risk of pests and diseases.
- **Air Purification:** More plants mean improved air quality. Vertical gardens contribute to better air purification and the reduction of urban heat island effects.

4. Plant Selection:

The choice of plants is crucial in vertical gardening. Consider the following factors when selecting plants:

- **Growth Habit:** Choose plants that naturally have a compact or trailing growth habit, as these are well-suited for vertical gardening. Climbing plants are also ideal.
- **Light Requirements:** Assess the light conditions in your space to select plants that will thrive in the available sunlight.

- **Maintenance Needs:** Opt for low-maintenance plants to make your vertical garden more manageable.
- **Edible Plants:** Vertical gardens are excellent for growing herbs, salad greens, and even small fruits or vegetables.

5. Maintenance:

Proper maintenance is essential to keep your vertical garden looking its best. Regularly check for watering needs, prune overgrowth, and inspect for pests and diseases. Fertilize as needed and be prepared to replace plants if they become unmanageable or unhealthy.

6. DIY or Pre-Made Solutions:

You can either create your own vertical garden structure or opt for pre-made solutions. DIY projects allow for customization and creativity, while pre-made systems often come with built-in irrigation and design features.

7. Sustainability:

Vertical gardening promotes sustainability by utilizing small spaces for productive gardening. It also contributes to improved air quality and reduced urban heat island effects. Additionally, growing your own herbs and vegetables can reduce your carbon footprint by reducing the need for store-bought produce.

8. Overcoming Challenges:

Vertical gardening isn't without its challenges. Ensuring adequate irrigation and managing plant growth are key concerns. Some plants may require more frequent care than traditional ground gardens, so be prepared to invest time in maintenance.

Color Schemes and Aesthetics

In balcony gardening, the role of aesthetics and color schemes cannot be understated. The careful selection of colors in your plant choices and decor can transform your outdoor space into a visually pleasing oasis.

By understanding the principles of color and design, you can create a balcony garden that evokes specific moods, reflects your personal style, and harmonizes with the surrounding environment.

Colors are not just visual stimuli; they have psychological and emotional effects. When choosing a color scheme for your balcony garden, it's essential to consider how different colors can impact the ambiance and overall feel of your space. Here's a glimpse into the emotional impact of common garden colors:

- **Green:** The color of nature, green creates a sense of calm and tranquility. It's a dominant color in most gardens and is often associated with growth, renewal, and relaxation.
- **Blue:** Blue is known for its calming and cooling effects. It evokes feelings of serenity and peace and can be an excellent choice for a space where you want to unwind and escape the urban hustle and bustle.

- **Yellow:** Yellow is a cheerful and sunny color. It brings warmth and energy to your balcony, making it a great choice for creating a lively and inviting atmosphere.
- **Red:** Red is a bold and passionate color. It's attention-grabbing and can be used to add drama and intensity to your garden. However, it should be used sparingly as it can be overwhelming in large quantities.
- **Purple:** Purple is associated with luxury and creativity. It can add a touch of elegance to your space and create a sense of mystery and sophistication.
- **Orange:** Orange is a vibrant and energetic color. It's an excellent choice for adding a burst of enthusiasm and zest to your balcony.
- **White:** White represents purity and simplicity. It creates a clean and serene atmosphere, making it a popular choice for minimalist and modern garden designs.

- **Pink:** Pink is soft and feminine, creating a delicate and charming ambiance. It's an ideal choice for a romantic or whimsical garden.

Creating a Harmonious Color Scheme

The key to an aesthetically pleasing balcony garden is a well-thought-out color scheme. Consider these guidelines for creating a harmonious color scheme:

1. The Color Wheel:

Understanding the color wheel is fundamental to creating a harmonious color scheme. It consists of primary colors (red, blue, and yellow), secondary colors (green, orange, and purple), and tertiary colors (combinations of primary and secondary colors).

Complementary colors, which are opposite each other on the color wheel (e.g., red and green or blue and orange), create high-contrast and visually stimulating combinations. Analogous colors, which are adjacent to each other on the color wheel (e.g., blue and green or red and orange), create a harmonious and soothing effect.

2. The 60-30-10 Rule:

A popular interior design guideline, the 60-30-10 rule, can also be applied to balcony gardening. It suggests that you should use one color for 60% of your design, another for 30%, and a third accent color for 10%. This creates a balanced and visually appealing composition.

3. Consider the Surrounding Environment:

Your balcony is not an isolated space. Consider the colors of the surrounding buildings, the sky, and the urban landscape. Harmonizing your color scheme with the environment can create a more integrated and cohesive garden.

4. Adapt to Your Space and Style:

Your choice of color should align with your personal style and the space's purpose. A minimalistic design may favor a monochromatic scheme with subtle variations, while a vibrant and lively garden may benefit from a rich and diverse palette.

5. Seasonal Changes:

Think about how your color scheme may change with the seasons. Some plants may bloom in different colors at different times of the year, allowing you to embrace seasonal diversity.

6. Foliage and Flowers:

Don't forget that foliage can contribute as much to your color scheme as flowers. Evergreen plants and ornamental foliage can provide consistent color, while flowering plants add dynamic changes to the palette.

7. Aesthetic Accents:

Beyond plant choices, consider using colorful decor and accessories, such as cushions, planters, pots, and furniture, to enhance your color scheme.

8. Experiment and Adapt:

Remember that color in gardening is not permanent. If you're not satisfied with your initial color scheme, don't hesitate to experiment and make changes. Gardening is a dynamic and evolving process.

Incorporating Furniture and Decor

When designing a balcony garden, it's essential to go beyond plants and containers to create a welcoming and functional outdoor space. Furniture and decor play a vital role in enhancing the aesthetics, comfort, and usability of your balcony. By thoughtfully incorporating these elements, you can transform your limited outdoor area into a cozy retreat, an entertainment space, or a tranquil haven for relaxation. In this article, we'll explore the art of incorporating furniture and decor into your balcony garden.

1. Choose Functional Furniture:

Selecting the right furniture is a critical step in creating a balcony garden that's both practical and visually appealing. Consider the following factors when choosing furniture:

- **Size and Scale:** Ensure that your furniture fits comfortably within the available space. Opt for pieces that don't overwhelm the balcony or make it feel cramped.
- **Comfort:** Comfort is key. Choose furniture with well-cushioned seats and backrests for a cozy and inviting atmosphere.

- **Durability:** Your balcony furniture will be exposed to the elements. Choose weather-resistant materials like metal, aluminum, or synthetic rattan that can withstand sun, rain, and wind.
- **Folding or Stackable:** If space is limited, consider foldable or stackable furniture that can be easily stored when not in use.
- **Style:** Select furniture that complements your overall design scheme. Modern, minimalist, rustic, and eclectic styles are just a few options to consider.
- **Purpose:** Determine the primary purpose of your balcony space. Do you want a dining area, a cozy reading nook, or a place to entertain guests? Let the intended use guide your furniture choices.

2. Cozy Seating Arrangements:

Creating a comfortable seating arrangement is the foundation of a functional balcony garden. Here are some ideas:

- **Bistro Sets:** Perfect for small balconies, bistro sets consist of a small table and two chairs. They're ideal for enjoying a morning coffee or a romantic dinner.

- **Lounge Chairs:** Lounge chairs or chaise lounges can turn your balcony into a space for relaxation and sunbathing. Consider adding cushions and throws for added comfort.
- **Sectional Sofas:** If space allows, a sectional sofa offers versatile seating arrangements. You can configure it to fit the shape of your balcony and add a coffee table for drinks or snacks.
- **Hammocks and Swings:** Hanging chairs, hammocks, or swing seats can be a whimsical addition, creating a laid-back and fun atmosphere.

3. Dining Areas:

If you'd like to dine on your balcony, consider the following options:

- **Dining Tables:** Choose a compact dining table that accommodates the number of people you intend to seat. Round tables are often a space-saving choice.
- **Folding Tables:** For ultimate space efficiency, folding tables can be stowed away when not in use.

- **Bar-Height Tables:** These tall tables and stools can create a casual and stylish outdoor bar atmosphere.
- **Cushioned Seating:** Pair your dining table with cushioned chairs or benches for a comfortable dining experience.

4. Decor Elements:

Decor elements add personality and style to your balcony garden. Here are some ideas:

- **Cushions and Pillows:** Colorful cushions and throw pillows can liven up your furniture and make your balcony feel cozier.
- **Outdoor Rugs:** Outdoor rugs can define your seating or dining area and add a touch of luxury to your balcony.
- **Lighting:** Consider string lights, lanterns, or wall-mounted fixtures to illuminate your space in the evening. Lighting adds ambiance and functionality.
- **Plant Stands and Shelves:** Incorporate plant stands or wall-mounted shelves to display your plant collection and bring your garden to eye level.

- **Artwork and Wall Decor:** Hang outdoor-friendly art or mirrors to add interest and personality to your balcony.
- **Water Features:** Small water fountains or tabletop water features can create a soothing atmosphere with the sound of running water.

5. Privacy Screens:

In urban settings, privacy can be a concern. Use privacy screens, trellises, or climbing plants to create a secluded and intimate environment on your balcony.

6. Multifunctional Furniture:

Consider furniture that serves multiple purposes. For example, a storage bench can provide seating while also offering a place to store gardening tools or outdoor cushions.

7. Green Decor:

Incorporate decor elements that complement the lushness of your garden, such as plant-themed wall art, decorative planters, or floral-patterned cushions.

8. Seasonal Decor:

Change your decor with the seasons. For instance, incorporate autumnal colors and pumpkins in the fall or add holiday lights and decorations during the winter holidays.

Maintaining Accessibility and Safety

While the primary focus of balcony gardening is to create a lush and visually appealing outdoor space, it's equally crucial to prioritize accessibility and safety. Ensuring that your balcony garden is easy to navigate and free from hazards is essential for both your enjoyment and the well-being of anyone who uses the space.

1. Clear Pathways:

Accessibility starts with maintaining clear pathways on your balcony. You should be able to move around without obstacles or tripping hazards. Here's how to achieve this:

- Arrange furniture and planters in a way that leaves ample space for walking. Ensure there's a clear path to all doors and exit points.

- Regularly inspect your balcony for any objects or debris that could block the way, such as fallen leaves or broken pots.
- Pay attention to trailing vines and overhanging branches, which can impede movement. Train these plants to grow upwards or prune them as needed.

2. Balcony Railings:

Safety is paramount, and one of the most critical safety features on your balcony is the railing. Ensure that the railing:

- **Is in good condition:** Regularly inspect the balcony railing for any signs of damage, corrosion, or instability. Make repairs or replacements as necessary.
- **Meets building codes:** Verify that your balcony railing complies with local building codes and safety standards, especially if you live in an apartment building or a condominium.
- **Has childproofing:** If you have young children or pets, install childproofing measures to prevent them from climbing or slipping through the railing.

-   **Is properly maintained:** Regularly clean and maintain the railing to prevent rust, mold, or other issues.

3. Furniture Stability:

The furniture on your balcony should be sturdy and secure. Consider the following:

-   Choose furniture with a low center of gravity to minimize the risk of tipping over in strong winds.
-   Secure lightweight or foldable furniture during windy conditions or storms.
-   Inspect furniture for loose screws, bolts, or wobbly legs, and tighten or repair them as needed.
-   Anchor tall furniture or items that could tip over in high winds to prevent accidents.

4. Slip-Resistant Surfaces:

Wet or moss-covered surfaces can become slippery and dangerous. Ensure your balcony has slip-resistant features:

-   Use outdoor rugs with non-slip backings to provide traction and reduce the risk of slipping.

- Regularly clean your balcony to remove moss, algae, or other substances that can make surfaces slick.
- Apply non-slip coatings or treatments to surfaces that are prone to becoming slippery.

5. Fire Safety:

Fire safety is a critical concern for balcony gardening. Follow these precautions:

- Avoid overloading your balcony with flammable materials or overcrowding it with plants and decor.
- Store propane tanks and other flammable materials in designated outdoor storage areas, away from direct sunlight and heat.
- Equip your balcony with fire extinguishers or a garden hose for immediate access in case of fire emergencies.

6. Child and Pet Safety:

If you have children or pets, it's essential to create a safe environment for them:

- Install childproofing measures, such as locks or barriers, to keep children from accessing areas of the balcony that may be unsafe.
- Choose plants that are non-toxic to pets and position them out of your pets' reach.
- Avoid using chemicals, such as pesticides or fertilizers, that could harm children or pets.

7. Maintenance Routines:

Create a regular maintenance routine to ensure the ongoing safety and accessibility of your balcony garden. This includes:

- Regularly inspecting all elements of your balcony, from the railing and furniture to the floor and plants.
- Trimming and pruning your plants to prevent overgrowth that can block pathways and create hazards.
- Cleaning your balcony surfaces to remove debris and prevent slipping.
- Addressing any maintenance or repair needs promptly to prevent further damage or safety risks.

8. Accessibility for All:

If you or any regular users of the balcony have mobility concerns or disabilities, ensure that the space is accessible to all. This may involve:

- Installing ramps or lifts for wheelchair access.
- Using containers and garden features that are reachable from a seated position.
- Making sure that the pathway is wide enough for wheelchair or walker use.

9. Emergency Preparedness:

In case of emergencies or evacuations, make sure you have a clear plan for safely exiting your balcony garden. Ensure that your garden does not obstruct access to doors or exits.

CHAPTER FOUR

Cultivating Your Balcony Garden

Amidst the bustling streets, towering skyscrapers, and the ceaseless rhythm of urban life, a unique and enchanting world awaits your discovery. It's a world where the confines of city living surrender to the vibrant allure of nature. This world is your very own balcony garden, an oasis suspended above the urban jungle, a sanctuary where the art of cultivation becomes a testament to the resilience of life in the midst of a concrete wilderness.

Cultivating a balcony garden is an art, a science, and a passionate endeavor that transforms a mere outdoor space into a thriving ecosystem, a place of rejuvenation, and a testament to the boundless beauty that nature bestows. It's an invitation to embark on a journey of growth, creativity, and discovery that transcends the limitations of space, bringing the outdoors to your doorstep.

In this bustling world, balconies are sacred spaces, often underutilized and neglected. They're the blank canvases upon which the enchanting story of your garden will unfold.

This introduction sets the stage for your journey into the enchanting world of balcony gardening, where we will explore the principles, strategies, and creative techniques that will help you turn your modest balcony into a lush, vibrant, and visually captivating garden.

The Urban Balcony as a Canvas

Your balcony, whether it's a small urban balcony or a more spacious one, offers untold potential to create a garden of exquisite beauty. It's a living canvas, a stage waiting for your creativity to come to life. Regardless of its size or layout, your balcony possesses a world of potential, where you can craft your green dreams.

From Limitations to Possibilities

Balcony gardening is an extraordinary art form that defies spatial constraints. While traditional gardens are tethered to the ground, balcony gardens transcend these limitations, introducing a vertical dimension to gardening. This dimension provides creative possibilities—think hanging gardens, wall-mounted planters, trellises, shelves, and other ingenious solutions that maximize both your floor and wall space.

It's a world of potential waiting to be explored, offering solutions that adapt to your space rather than the other way around.

Personal Expression and Purpose

Designing and nurturing a balcony garden is a deeply personal and purposeful endeavor. It's a unique opportunity to express your style, preferences, and personality through the arrangement of plants, colors, and decor. As you embark on this journey, consider the ambiance you wish to create. Do you envision a serene retreat with aromatic herbs and calming colors, or a vibrant space bursting with flowering plants and vivid hues? The possibilities are as diverse as the individuals who embark on this adventure.

Gardening with Intent

Balcony gardening is more than just a pastime; it's an expression of intent. Your garden can serve various purposes, catering to your specific goals and interests. Are you an aspiring chef who longs for a bounty of herbs and vegetables at your fingertips? Or perhaps you seek a fragrant sanctuary filled with aromatic blooms and soothing herbs.

Your balcony garden can also play a vital role in conserving the environment, providing a refuge for pollinators and helping to reduce the heat of the urban landscape.

The Importance of Design

Balcony garden design is about more than just arranging plants; it's a careful orchestration of elements that create a harmonious and balanced space. It involves considering the layout, the choice of containers, the selection of plants, color schemes, and the interplay of light and shade. Effective design ensures that your garden not only looks beautiful but also functions optimally, fostering plant health and growth.

Urban Gardening with Purpose

Balcony gardening is not just a personal endeavor; it's also an essential step in urban gardening with purpose. Balcony gardens contribute to air purification, carbon sequestration, and urban heat reduction. They can also serve as vital stepping stones for pollinators in an otherwise challenging urban environment.

Navigating Challenges

Balcony gardening is not without its unique challenges. From limited space and varying sunlight exposure to potential pest issues, these challenges are all part of the journey. However, with knowledge, creative solutions, and a passion for plants, these challenges can be navigated successfully.

In the exploration of balcony garden cultivation, you will discover how to make the most of your space, create a garden that aligns with your vision, and embrace the changing seasons as opportunities for growth and transformation.

By the end of this journey, you'll have the tools and inspiration needed to turn your balcony into a thriving urban oasis—a place where you can escape, connect with nature, and celebrate the beauty of life amid the city's hustle and bustle.

Balcony gardening is an invitation to embark on a fulfilling and creative journey, one that will reward you with the joys of cultivating life and beauty high above the urban landscape.

It's an opportunity to experience the peace and serenity of nature in the heart of the city, an oasis suspended above the urban jungle where the wonders of the natural world become part of your daily life.

Planting and Transplanting Techniques

Planting and transplanting are fundamental aspects of balcony gardening, and mastering these techniques is crucial to the success of your garden. Whether you're starting from seeds, young seedlings, or mature plants, knowing how to plant and transplant effectively will ensure that your garden thrives. In this guide, we'll explore the essential planting and transplanting techniques to help you create a flourishing and vibrant balcony garden.

1. Selecting Containers:

Choosing the right containers is the first step in successful planting and transplanting. Consider the following factors:

- Size: Ensure the container is appropriately sized for the plants you intend to grow. Smaller containers are ideal for herbs and small annuals, while larger ones are better suited for shrubs or vegetables.

- **Drainage:** Proper drainage is essential to prevent waterlogged soil, which can lead to root rot. Containers should have drainage holes in the bottom to allow excess water to escape.
- **Material:** Containers come in various materials, such as plastic, ceramic, terracotta, and wood. Each material has its advantages and considerations. Plastic containers are lightweight and retain moisture well, while terracotta allows for better aeration but may require more frequent watering.

2. Soil Selection:

Quality soil is a cornerstone of successful gardening. Choose a potting mix that is well-draining and enriched with organic matter. You can also customize your soil mix to suit the specific needs of your plants. For example, herbs and succulents benefit from a well-draining mix, while vegetables may require a richer, nutrient-dense soil.

3. Starting from Seeds:

If you're starting your plants from seeds, follow these steps:

- Fill your containers with potting mix, leaving a little space at the top for watering.
- Plant the seeds according to the recommended depth on the seed packet.
- Gently water the soil to ensure good seed-to-soil contact, and cover the containers with plastic wrap or a clear plastic lid to create a mini-greenhouse effect.
- Place the containers in a warm, well-lit location (a south-facing balcony is ideal) and maintain consistent moisture levels.
- Once the seedlings have sprouted and developed their first true leaves, thin them out to allow the healthiest ones to grow.
- Transplant the seedlings to larger containers as they outgrow their current space.

4. Transplanting Seedlings:

Transplanting seedlings is a delicate process that requires care to avoid damaging the young plants. Follow these steps:

- Water the seedlings thoroughly before transplanting to help the soil hold together.
- Gently remove the seedlings from their current container by pressing on the bottom of the pot or using a small stick to ease them out.
- Create a hole in the new container's soil for each seedling. The hole should be deep enough to accommodate the root system and slightly wider than the seedling's root ball.
- Carefully place each seedling into its hole, ensuring the roots are spread out and not crowded. Press the soil gently around the seedling to secure it in place.
- Water the transplanted seedlings to settle the soil and hydrate the roots. Avoid overwatering, as this can lead to root rot.

5. Transplanting Mature Plants

When moving mature plants to a new container, follow these steps:

- Water the plant thoroughly a day or two before transplanting. Well-hydrated roots are more resilient during the transplant process.

- Choose a container that is larger than the current one but not too oversized, as excess soil can retain moisture and cause root rot.
- Gently remove the mature plant from its current container. This may require tapping the sides or sliding a knife along the edges to loosen the root ball.
- Place the plant in the new container, ensuring that it sits at the same depth as it did in the original container. Fill in the space with fresh potting mix.
- Water the plant thoroughly, allowing the soil to settle around the roots. Avoid compacting the soil too much, as it can hinder water and air circulation.

6. Care After Transplanting

After transplanting, monitor your plants closely for signs of stress, such as wilting or yellowing leaves. To minimize stress:

- Keep your plants well-watered in the days following transplanting, as they may experience shock.
- Provide the appropriate light conditions for your plants, whether they require full sun, partial sun, or shade.

- Fertilize your plants according to their specific needs, using a balanced, water-soluble fertilizer.
- Inspect your plants for any signs of pests or diseases, addressing any issues promptly.

Proper Care and Maintenance

A thriving balcony garden is a testament to your nurturing care and dedication. Proper care and maintenance are the cornerstones of a flourishing garden, ensuring that your plants grow vibrantly, bloom beautifully, and stay healthy throughout the changing seasons.

1. Regular Watering:

Balcony plants rely on you for their water needs. Here are some key watering tips:

- **Consistency:** Establish a regular watering routine based on the needs of your plants. Some may require daily watering, while others can go a few days without.
- **Watering Technique:** Water your plants at the base to avoid wetting the foliage, which can lead to mold and disease.

Water until you see excess water draining from the bottom of the container, ensuring that the roots are adequately hydrated.

- **Monitor Soil Moisture:** To determine when it's time to water, insert your finger into the soil. If it's dry to the touch about an inch below the surface, it's time to water.

- **Consider Self-Watering Systems:** Self-watering containers or irrigation systems can help maintain consistent moisture levels, making it easier to care for your garden.

2. Fertilizing:

Balcony plants may deplete the nutrients in their containers over time. To replenish these nutrients, use the following guidelines:

- **Balanced Fertilizer:** Use a balanced, water-soluble fertilizer that contains essential macro and micronutrients. Follow the manufacturer's recommendations for application frequency and dilution.

- **Avoid Over-Fertilizing:** Over-fertilization can lead to nutrient imbalances, root damage, and excessive foliage growth at the expense of flowers or fruit. Stick to the recommended dosage.
- **Seasonal Adjustments:** Adjust your fertilization routine according to the growing season. Many plants benefit from a higher frequency of feeding during their active growth periods and reduced feeding during the dormant season.

3. Pruning and Deadheading

Pruning and deadheading are essential for promoting healthy growth and a neat appearance:

- **Deadheading:** Remove spent flowers to encourage new blooms and prevent energy from going into seed production.
- **Pruning:** Regularly trim back leggy or overgrown growth to maintain the desired shape and size of your plants. Pruning also helps improve air circulation and reduces the risk of disease.

4. Pest and Disease Management

Balcony gardens are not immune to pests and diseases. Effective pest and disease management involves the following steps:

- **Early Detection:** Regularly inspect your plants for signs of pests or disease. Catching issues early makes them easier to manage.
- **Organic Remedies:** When possible, use organic pest control methods, such as neem oil, insecticidal soap, or natural predators, to keep pests in check.
- **Isolation:** If you detect pests or diseases on one plant, consider isolating it to prevent the issue from spreading to other plants.
- **Prune Affected Areas:** If a portion of a plant is severely affected, consider pruning that section to prevent the problem from spreading.

5. Seasonal Care

Balcony gardens experience the changing seasons, and your care routine should adapt accordingly:

- **Winter Protection:** In cold climates, protect your plants from freezing temperatures by bringing them indoors, covering them, or using frost cloth.
- **Summer Sunscreen:** During scorching summers, provide shade for plants that prefer indirect sunlight. This can be achieved with shade cloth or by relocating plants as needed.
- **Seasonal Transitions:** When transitioning plants indoors or outdoors with the changing seasons, acclimate them gradually to prevent shock.

6. Soil Maintenance:

Balcony garden soil needs periodic attention to stay healthy:

- **Replenish Nutrients:** Over time, the soil in containers may become depleted. Add fresh potting mix or compost as needed to replenish nutrients.
- **Aeration:** Regularly aerate the soil to improve drainage and root health. Gently loosen the top layer of soil with a hand rake or small cultivator.
- **Top Dressing:** Apply a layer of organic mulch on the soil surface to retain moisture, regulate temperature, and reduce weed growth.

7. Container Care:

The containers themselves require attention to ensure they remain functional and attractive:

- **Cleaning:** Periodically clean the containers to remove algae, mold, or mineral deposits. A mix of water and vinegar can be effective for cleaning.
- **Repotting:** As plants grow and outgrow their containers, repot them into larger containers with fresh soil. This allows for continued healthy growth.
- **Container Replacement:** Over time, containers may become damaged or deteriorate. Replace containers as needed to maintain the integrity of your garden.

Pruning and Deadheading for Healthier Plants

Pruning and deadheading are essential techniques for maintaining the health and vibrancy of your garden. These practices involve the selective removal of plant parts, such as branches, stems, or spent flowers, and are crucial for encouraging new growth, improving air circulation, and preventing disease.

When applied correctly, pruning and deadheading can rejuvenate your plants, enhance their appearance, and extend their lifespan..

Pruning: The Art of Shaping and Training

Pruning is the intentional removal of certain plant parts to promote healthy growth, control size, and improve structure. Whether you're dealing with flowering plants, shrubs, or trees, proper pruning can work wonders for your garden.

When to Prune:

The timing of pruning largely depends on the type of plant and its growth habits:

- **Winter Pruning:** Many deciduous trees and shrubs are pruned during late winter or early spring when they are dormant. This allows for easier visibility of the plant's structure and minimizes stress on the plant.
- **Spring Pruning:** Some early-blooming shrubs, like forsythia or lilac, should be pruned shortly after flowering in the spring. This timing allows them to produce new growth for the following year's blossoms.

- **Summer Pruning:** For many plants, especially those that flower in late spring or early summer, summer pruning is ideal. Pruning during this time encourages new growth and helps maintain the plant's shape.
- **Autumn Pruning:** Pruning in the fall is generally discouraged, as it may stimulate new growth that won't have sufficient time to harden off before winter. However, it can be done for specific reasons, such as removing dead or diseased branches.

Pruning Goals:

The primary goals of pruning are to:

- **Remove Dead or Diseased Material:** Prune away dead, damaged, or diseased branches to prevent the spread of disease and allow the plant to allocate energy to healthy growth.
- **Improve Structure:** Enhance the overall shape and structure of the plant, removing any crossed or rubbing branches and encouraging a more open form.
- **Encourage New Growth:** Promote new growth and flowering by removing old or spent blooms and shaping the plant for optimal sunlight exposure.

- **Control Size:** Manage the size of your plant to fit your space and keep it in proportion with other garden elements.
- **Thinning:** Thinning out branches and foliage increases air circulation, reducing the risk of fungal diseases and pest infestations.

Pruning Techniques

When pruning, it's crucial to use the right tools and techniques to avoid injuring the plant. Here are some key techniques:

- **Selective Pruning:** Rather than removing large sections of a branch, make precise cuts just above a leaf node or bud, which encourages new growth.
- **Clean Cuts:** Use sharp, clean pruning shears to make smooth cuts that minimize stress on the plant. Avoid tearing or crushing branches.
- **Prune at a 45-Degree Angle:** Make your cuts at a 45-degree angle, sloping away from the bud or node, to prevent water from collecting on the cut surface.

- **Sterilize Tools:** Sterilize your pruning tools before use to prevent the spread of diseases from one plant to another.

Deadheading: Promoting Continuous Bloom

Deadheading is the removal of spent flowers, a practice that encourages plants to produce more blooms. By preventing the plant from going to seed, it redirects its energy into producing new flowers, resulting in a more extended and prolific blooming period.

When to Deadhead

Deadheading should be performed throughout the growing season, particularly after the first flush of blooms has faded. The frequency depends on the plant and the number of flowers it produces.

Deadheading Techniques

To deadhead effectively:

- **Pinch or Snip:** Using your fingers or small pruning shears, pinch or snip the faded flower just below the spent bloom, above a leaf node or bud.

110

- **Remove Seed Heads:** For plants that produce seed heads, like marigolds or zinnias, remove the entire seed head to prevent self-seeding and promote new blooms.
- **Maintain Appearance:** Deadheading also helps keep your garden looking tidy and attractive by removing unsightly, withered flowers.

Benefits of Pruning and Deadheading

The benefits of proper pruning and deadheading are numerous:

- **Extended Bloom Period:** Regular deadheading results in continuous blooms, ensuring your garden remains vibrant throughout the growing season.
- **Enhanced Aesthetics:** Pruning and deadheading improve the appearance and shape of your plants, creating a more visually appealing garden.
- **Improved Health:** Removing dead or diseased material, as well as thinning out dense growth, promotes better air circulation and reduces the risk of pests and diseases.

- **Controlled Size:** Pruning allows you to control the size of your plants, keeping them in proportion with your garden space.
- **Stronger Growth:** By removing old, weak, or overgrown branches, pruning encourages healthier and more vigorous new growth.

Dealing with Common Challenges and Issues

Balcony gardening, while a rewarding and enriching hobby, is not without its share of common challenges and issues. Whether you're a seasoned gardener or just starting out, it's essential to be prepared for the common obstacles that may arise in your green oasis high above the urban landscape. By understanding and addressing these challenges, you can cultivate a healthier, more vibrant balcony garden.

1. Limited Space:

Balconies typically offer limited square footage, which can be a challenge when selecting and arranging plants. However, limited space doesn't have to limit your creativity. Here's how to deal with this challenge:

- **Vertical Gardening:** Make the most of your space by incorporating vertical gardening techniques, such as trellises, hanging planters, and wall-mounted shelves.
- **Select Compact Varieties:** Choose compact or dwarf varieties of plants that won't overwhelm your space. Many vegetables, herbs, and ornamental plants come in smaller versions ideal for small spaces.
- **Group Plants:** Arrange plants in groupings to create a lush, layered effect. This approach maximizes visual impact while conserving space.

2. Sunlight Limitations:

Balconies can be shaded by neighboring buildings or face the wrong direction for optimal sunlight. Here's how to address issues with sunlight:

- **Select Plants Wisely:** Choose plants that match your balcony's sunlight conditions. Some thrive in full sun, while others are more shade-tolerant.

- **Use Reflective Surfaces:** Position reflective surfaces, such as mirrors or light-colored walls, to bounce sunlight onto your plants, creating microclimates of better light.
- **Rotate Plants:** If your balcony receives partial sunlight, rotate your plants regularly to ensure they receive even light exposure.

3. Wind and Temperature Fluctuations:

Balconies are often exposed to strong winds and temperature fluctuations, which can stress and damage plants. To mitigate these challenges:

- **Windbreaks:** Erect windbreaks, such as outdoor curtains, lattice screens, or glass panels, to shield your plants from strong winds.
- **Monitor Temperatures:** Keep an eye on temperature changes and cover your plants during unexpected frosts or excessively hot days.
- **Hardy Plant Selection:** Choose plants that can withstand the temperature fluctuations in your region. Cold-hardy plants can endure colder winters, while heat-tolerant varieties can survive intense summer heat.

4. Pests and Diseases:

Pests and diseases can infiltrate your balcony garden. To combat these issues:

- **Regular Inspection:** Frequently inspect your plants for any signs of pests or diseases. Early detection allows for swift action.
- **Natural Predators:** Encourage beneficial insects, such as ladybugs and lacewings, which feed on garden pests. You can also introduce nematodes to the soil to control certain soil-dwelling pests.
- **Organic Pest Control:** Utilize organic pest control methods like neem oil, insecticidal soap, or diatomaceous earth to manage pest infestations.

5. Soil Quality:

Soil in containers can become depleted over time. Address soil quality concerns by:

- **Regularly Replenishing:** Periodically refresh your container soil by adding fresh potting mix or compost to ensure plants receive the nutrients they need.

- **Aeration:** Loosen the soil periodically to enhance drainage and root health. Avoid compaction that can hinder air circulation.

6. Watering Challenges:

Watering is a delicate balance in balcony gardening. Overwatering or underwatering can lead to plant stress. To manage watering effectively:

- **Consistent Schedule:** Establish a regular watering routine based on the needs of your plants. Pay attention to soil moisture levels to determine when watering is necessary.
- **Self-Watering Systems:** Consider using self-watering containers or irrigation systems to maintain consistent moisture levels and simplify watering tasks.

7. Maintenance and Accessibility:

Maintaining your balcony garden can be physically demanding, and accessibility can be a challenge. To address these issues:

- **Use the Right Tools:** Invest in lightweight and ergonomic gardening tools to ease maintenance tasks. Consider raised planters to reduce the need for bending or kneeling.
- **Safety Measures:** Ensure your balcony is safe and accessible for all users, including children and elderly family members or friends. Use childproofing measures if necessary.

8. Pest Control and Pesticides:

Balcony gardens are susceptible to pests, but the use of pesticides can harm both beneficial insects and the environment. To manage pests responsibly:

- **Integrated Pest Management:** Employ an integrated pest management approach, which combines prevention, monitoring, and control methods to minimize the use of pesticides.
- **Companion Planting:** Plant companion plants that naturally deter pests. For example, marigolds can help keep aphids away from your vegetable plants.

9. Seasonal Transitions:

Seasonal transitions can be a challenge when moving plants in and out of your balcony. To manage these transitions:

- **Gradual Acclimation:** Gradually acclimate plants to new outdoor or indoor conditions to minimize shock and stress during seasonal transitions.

10. Soil Erosion and Runoff:

Heavy rainfall or overwatering can lead to soil erosion and runoff on your balcony. To manage this:

- **Use Mulch:** Apply a layer of mulch on the soil surface to help control erosion and retain moisture.
- **Water Management:** Water your plants in moderation to prevent excessive runoff. Use saucers under containers to catch excess water and prevent damage to your balcony.

Harvesting and Enjoying the Fruits of Your Labor

As the seasons unfold, the diligent care and nurturing you invest in your balcony garden lead to the most gratifying moment: harvest time.

The joy of reaping the fruits of your labor, quite literally, is a delightful reward for the time and effort you've dedicated to your green sanctuary high above the city.

Harvesting with Precision

Timing is critical when it comes to harvesting your plants. The best time to harvest varies depending on the type of plant you are dealing with, and there are some general principles to keep in mind:

- **Fruits and Vegetables:** Harvest when they reach the ideal size and ripeness. This often means picking them just before they are fully ripe to allow for the ripening process to complete off the plant. Consult seed packets or plant labels for guidance on specific varieties.
- **Herbs:** Herbs are typically harvested when they have enough foliage to spare. The best time is usually before the plant flowers, as this is when they have the most flavor.

- **Flowers:** Cut flowers for bouquets when they are in full bloom but not wilting. The best time for harvesting varies by species, so familiarize yourself with the specific requirements of your flowers.
- **Seeds:** To harvest seeds for future planting, wait until the seed heads or pods begin to dry out on the plant. Collect them carefully and allow them to dry fully indoors before storing.
- **Leafy Greens:** Harvest leafy greens like lettuce, spinach, and chard when the leaves are young and tender. Regular harvesting encourages new growth and prolongs the harvest.

Tools for Harvesting

Equipping yourself with the right tools can make the harvesting process efficient and enjoyable. Here are some tools to consider:

- **Pruning Shears:** Ideal for cutting herbs, flowers, and small branches.
- **Harvesting Knife or Scissors:** Especially useful for collecting larger fruits and vegetables.

- **Gloves:** Protect your hands when handling prickly or thorny plants.

Harvesting Tips

To make your harvest as efficient and successful as possible, keep these tips in mind:

- **Harvest in the Morning:** For many plants, morning is the best time to harvest because the foliage is fully hydrated and crisp.
- **Avoid Overcrowding:** When harvesting, take care not to damage neighboring plants. Gently move leaves or branches aside to access the produce.
- **Handle with Care:** Delicate fruits and vegetables, like berries, should be handled gently to avoid bruising or damage.

Enjoying the Fruits of Your Labor

The joy of gardening isn't solely in the act of growing; it's also in savoring the fruits of your labor. Here are some delightful ways to enjoy what your balcony garden has to offer:

Culinary Creations

Balcony-grown produce adds freshness and flavor to your culinary endeavors. Incorporate your harvest into a variety of dishes, such as:

- **Salads:** Lettuce, spinach, and arugula are perfect for fresh salads. Add herbs like basil, mint, and parsley for added zing.
- **Fresh Herbs:** Infuse your dishes with the flavors of homegrown herbs, from basil and oregano to cilantro and thyme.
- **Vegetable Stir-Fries:** Use your homegrown veggies like bell peppers, snap peas, and cherry tomatoes for colorful stir-fries.
- **Salsas and Dips:** Whip up salsa with homegrown tomatoes, jalapeños, and onions, or create creamy herb dips.
- **Smoothies:** Blend homegrown berries, bananas, and fresh herbs into vibrant, nutritious smoothies.

Floral Arrangements

Your balcony blooms can be used to create beautiful floral arrangements that brighten your living space. Cut fresh flowers and arrange them in vases or containers to enhance your home's decor. Celebrate special occasions or simply uplift your surroundings with the beauty of your garden.

Homemade Gifts

Homemade gifts crafted with your balcony garden harvest are thoughtful and personal. Consider making homemade jams or preserves using your fruits, or create herb-infused oils and vinegars to share with friends and family.

Drying and Preserving

Extend the enjoyment of your harvest by drying or preserving some of your bounty. Here are a few preservation methods to explore:

- **Drying Herbs:** Hang or air-dry herbs like basil, oregano, or lavender to create dried herb jars for your kitchen.
- **Canning:** Preserve fruits and vegetables by canning them in jars to enjoy their flavors year-round.

- **Freezing:** Freeze excess produce like berries or herbs in airtight containers to use in recipes throughout the year.

Savoring the Season

Every season in your balcony garden brings new opportunities to savor the flavors and beauty of your harvest. Enjoy the sense of accomplishment that comes from growing your own food and the pride of using your homegrown herbs, flowers, and produce in your daily life.

The process of nurturing and harvesting your balcony garden is an enduring cycle, one that connects you to nature and sustains your spirit. From the first seed sown to the final harvest, your balcony garden embodies the cycle of life and growth, providing you with the joys of cultivation and a deeper appreciation of the natural world.

The fruits of your labor are not just a feast for the senses; they are a testament to your dedication and the enduring beauty that emerges from the heart of the urban jungle.

CONCLUSION

In the world of gardening, balcony gardening for beginners offers a uniquely accessible and rewarding start to what can become a lifelong journey of horticultural discovery. Whether you reside in a bustling city, suburban neighborhood, or even a rural setting, the allure of transforming your small outdoor space into a lush, green haven is both fulfilling and inspiring.

The essence of balcony gardening for beginners lies in the ability to adapt and create a flourishing oasis despite space constraints.

Throughout this guide, we have explored the essential elements of balcony gardening, from choosing the right containers and soil to selecting suitable plants, understanding sunlight and microclimates, and mastering the use of gardening tools and materials.

We've delved into the art of designing your balcony garden, optimizing space, and enhancing aesthetics while maintaining accessibility and safety.

We've also covered the intricacies of planting, transplanting, pruning, deadheading, and proper care to ensure the health and vibrancy of your garden.

As you embark on your balcony gardening journey, remember that every step, from preparing the soil to tending to your plants, is a form of connection with the natural world. It is a testament to your dedication and the enduring beauty that emerges from the heart of the urban jungle.

Balcony gardening offers an array of benefits, from providing fresh herbs, vegetables, and beautiful flowers to improving the environment and enhancing your well-being.

The satisfaction of nurturing life, witnessing the miracle of growth, and savoring the fruits of your labor is an experience that transcends the limitations of space and location.

Your balcony garden is more than just a collection of plants; it is a sanctuary that fosters a deep connection with the living world, a retreat from the urban hustle, and a testament to your ability to adapt and thrive in any environment.

So, as you venture into the world of balcony gardening for beginners, know that every challenge you face and every plant you tend is a step toward nurturing nature within a cityscape. Embrace the joy of growing, adapt to the unique conditions of your balcony, and create a space that not only reflects your personality but also adds a touch of greenery to your everyday life.

Whether you are a novice or an experienced gardener, your balcony garden is an ongoing experiment, a canvas of color, and a source of endless delight.

In the end, balcony gardening is not just about growing plants; it's about nurturing your connection to the earth, finding solace in the midst of urban life, and celebrating the beauty of life's simplest pleasures.

Balcony gardening for beginners is an invitation to embrace the art of cultivation, a journey that transforms your outdoor space into a flourishing haven, a testament to your green thumb and the enduring beauty that nature offers, even in the most compact of spaces.

Manufactured by Amazon.ca
Acheson, AB